THIS SCARY BOOK BELC

*Thank you for choosing our coloring book.
We hope that the pictures contained in it will
bring you a lot of fun while coloring.*

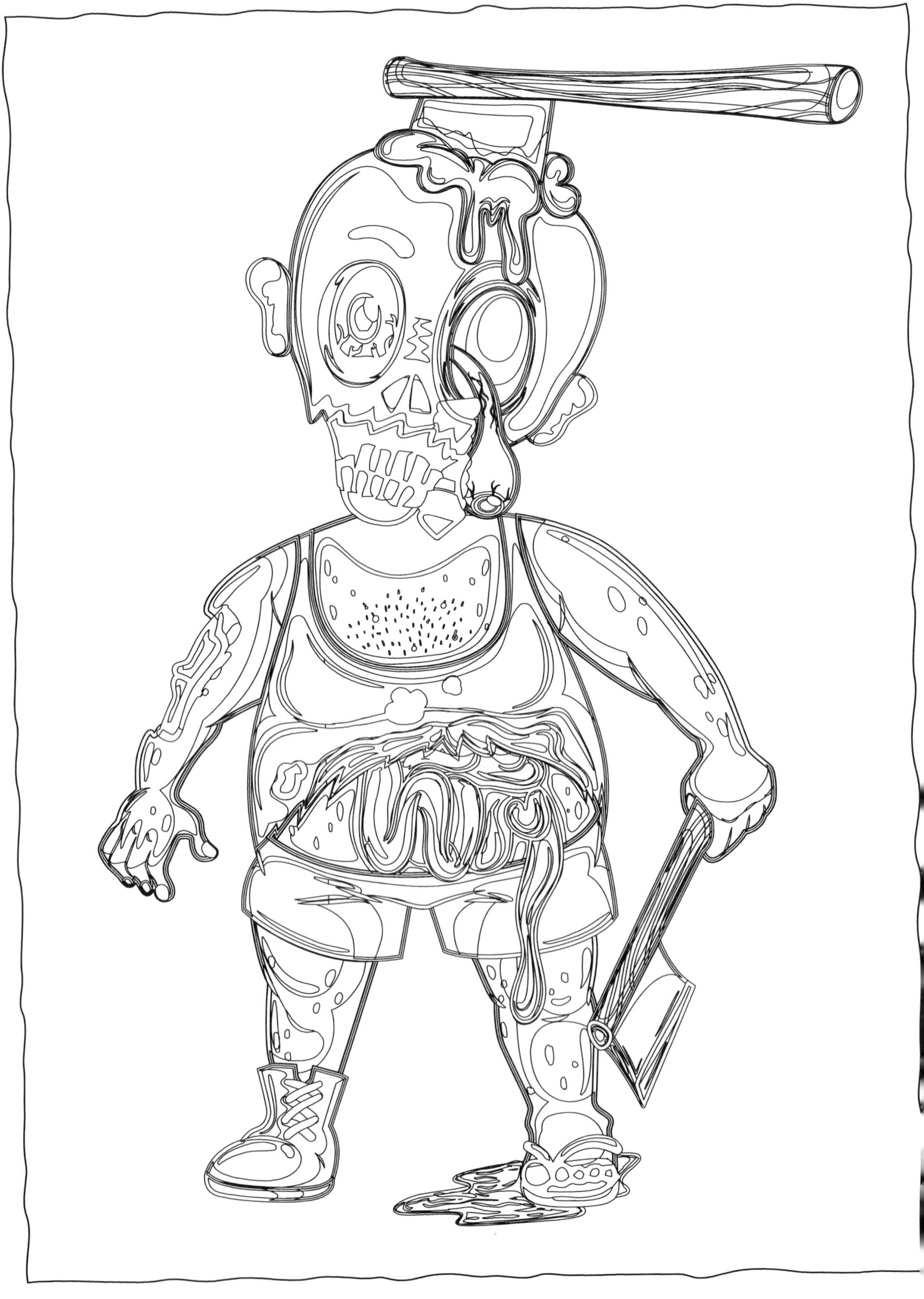

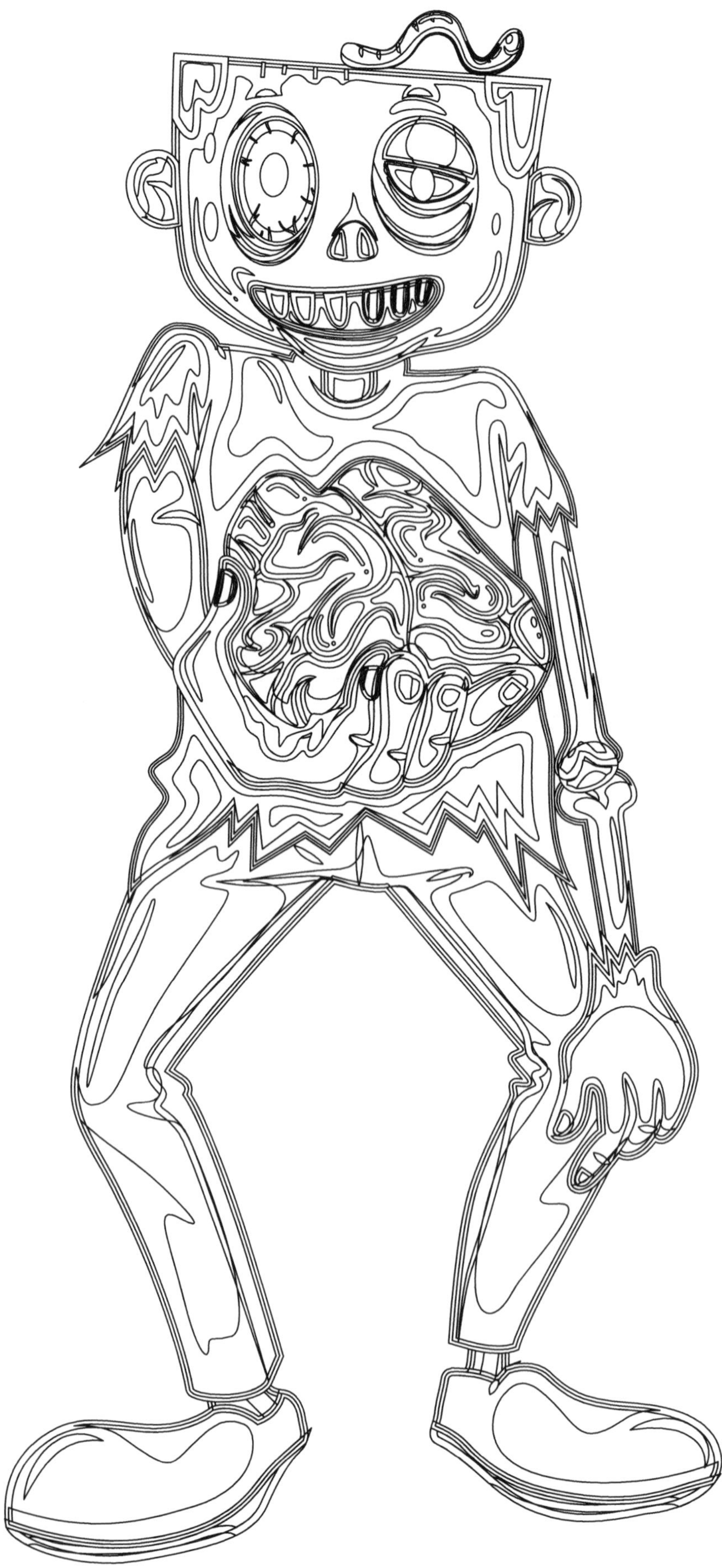

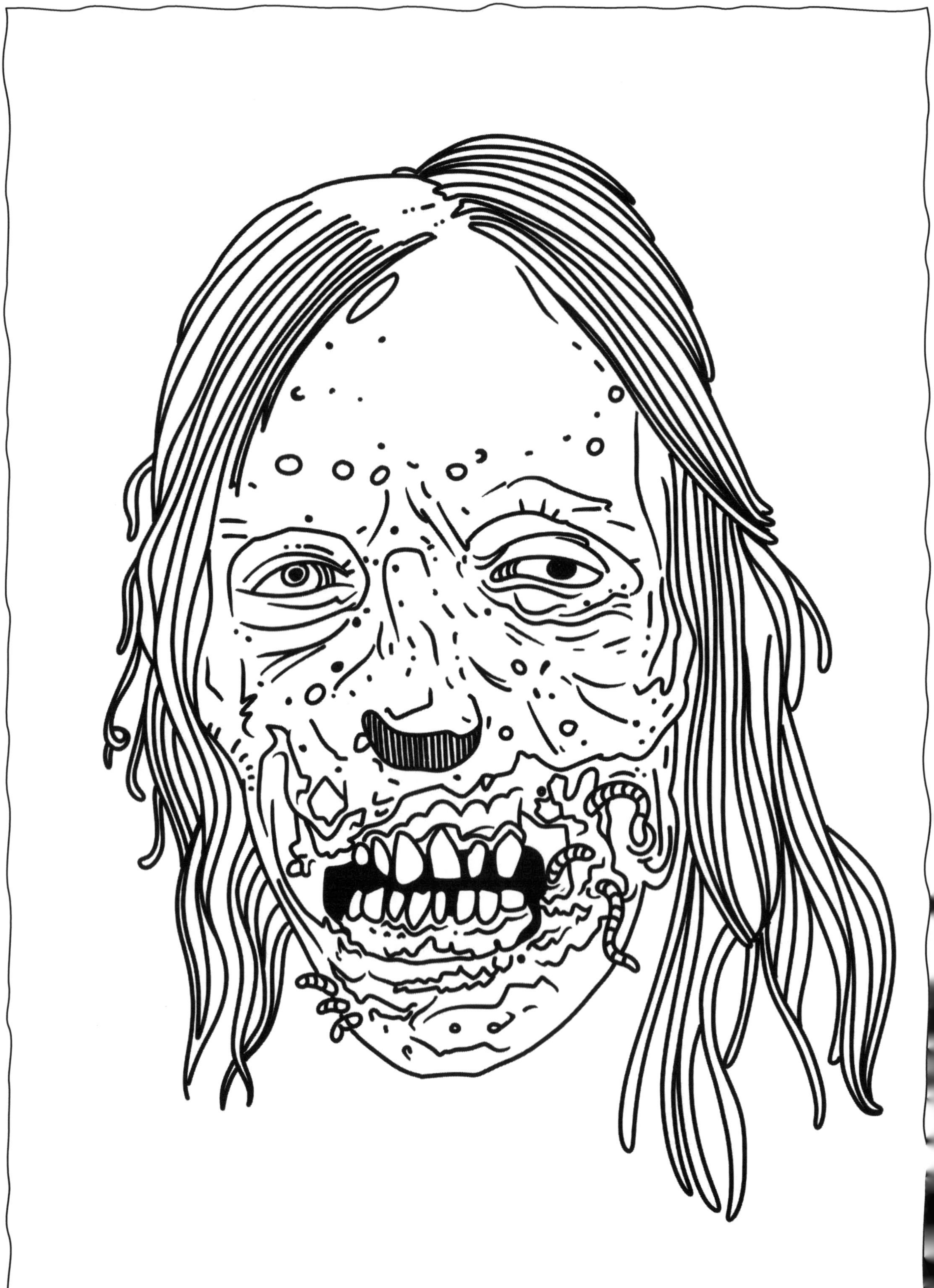

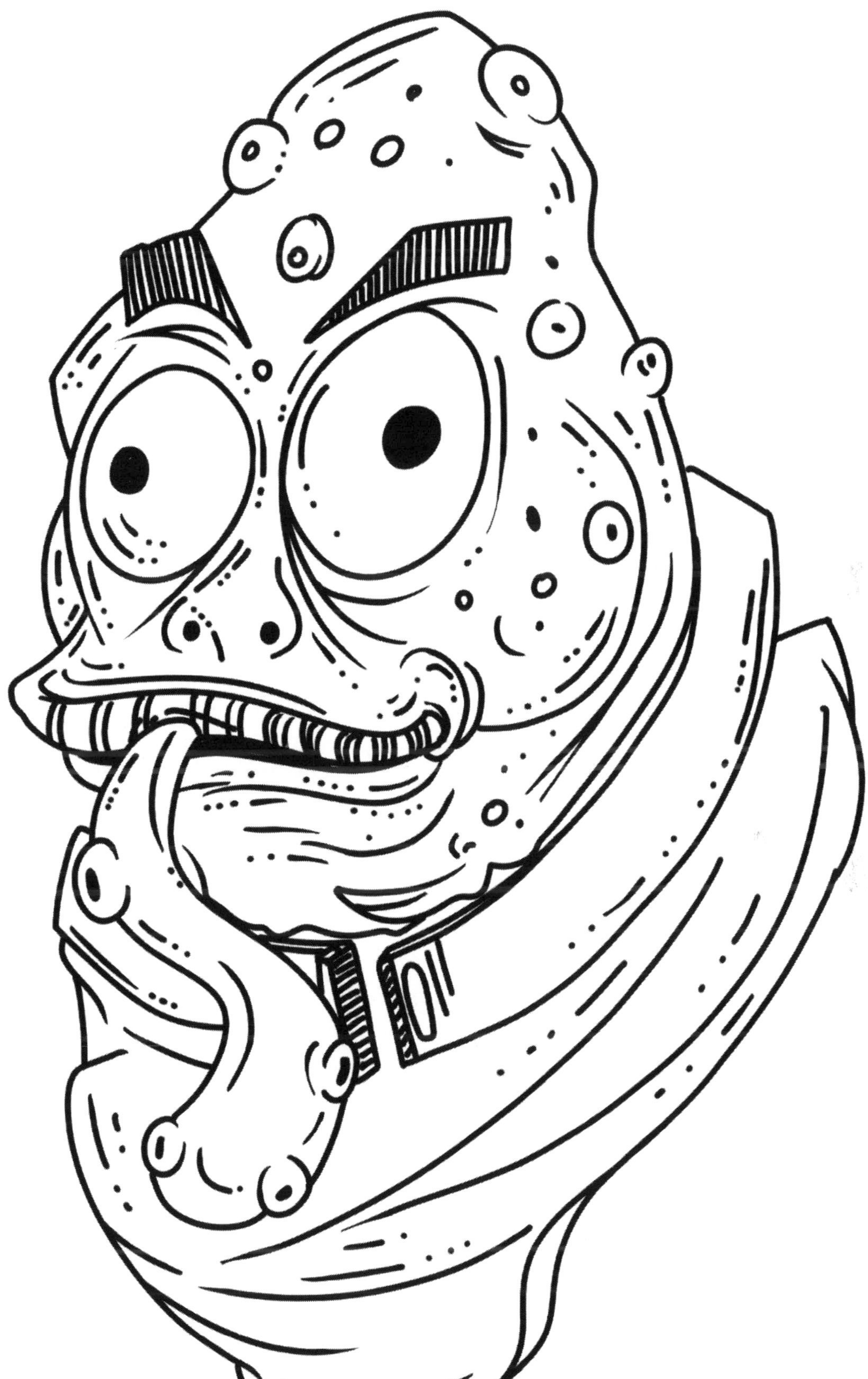

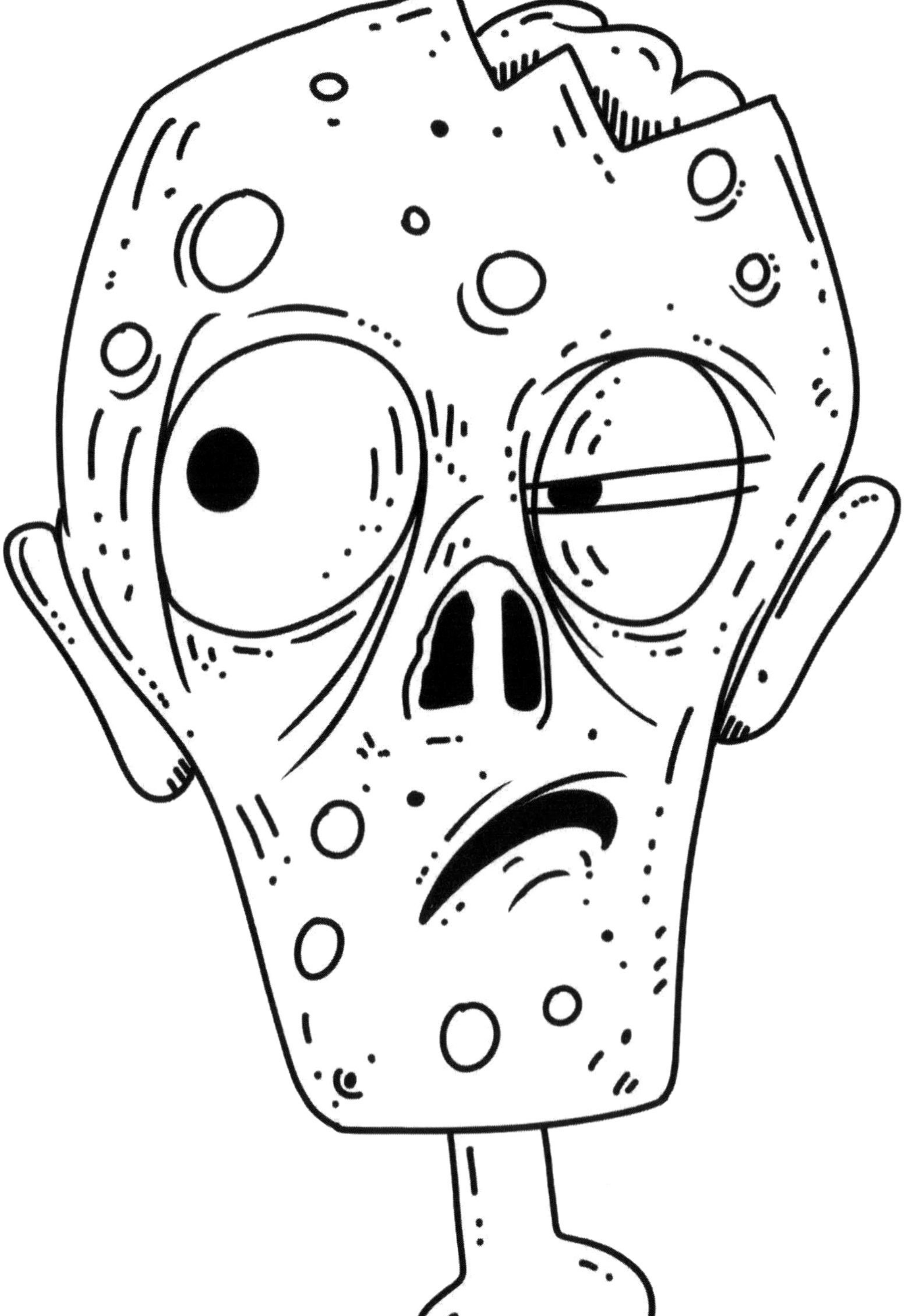

ZOMBIE CROSSING

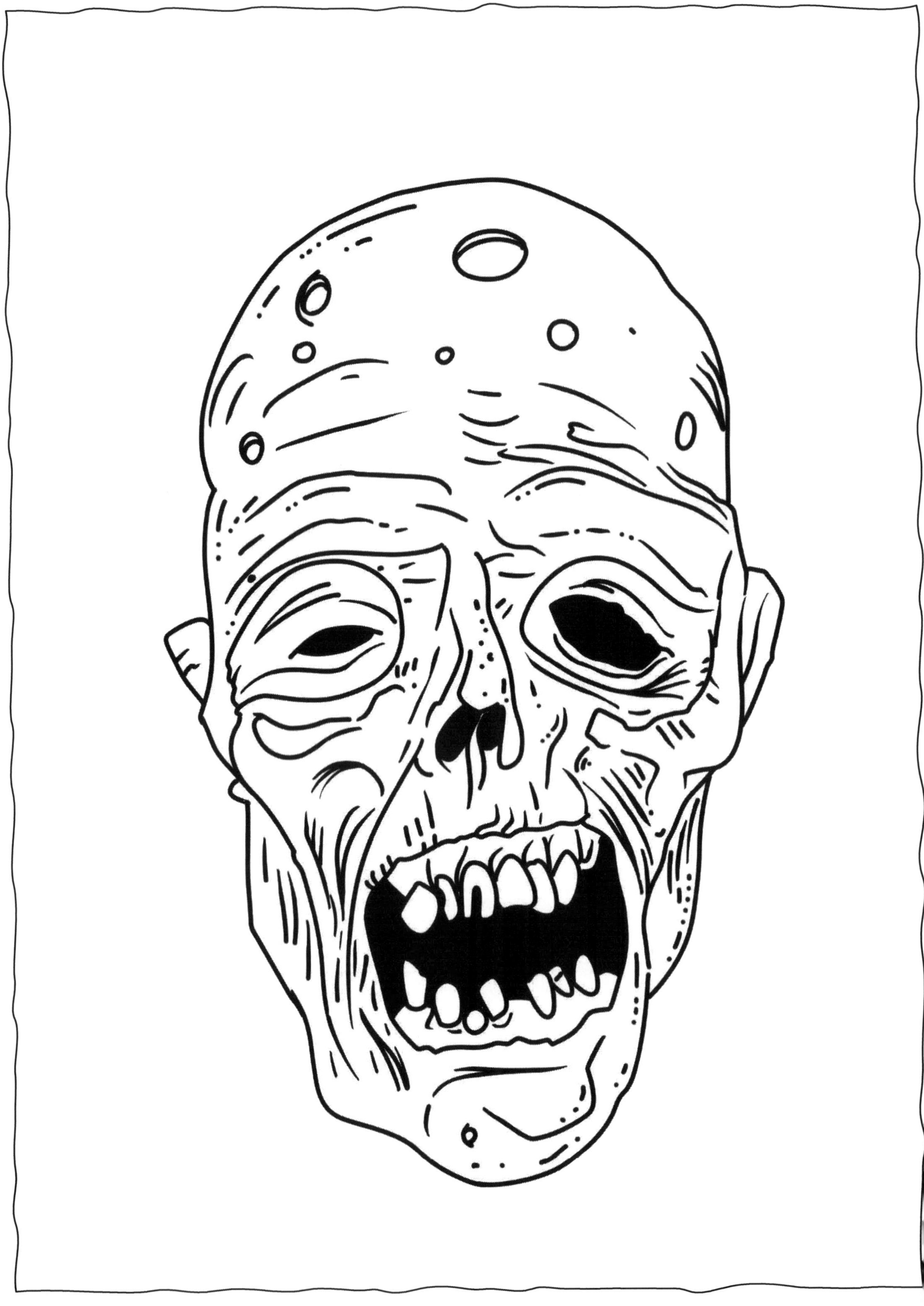

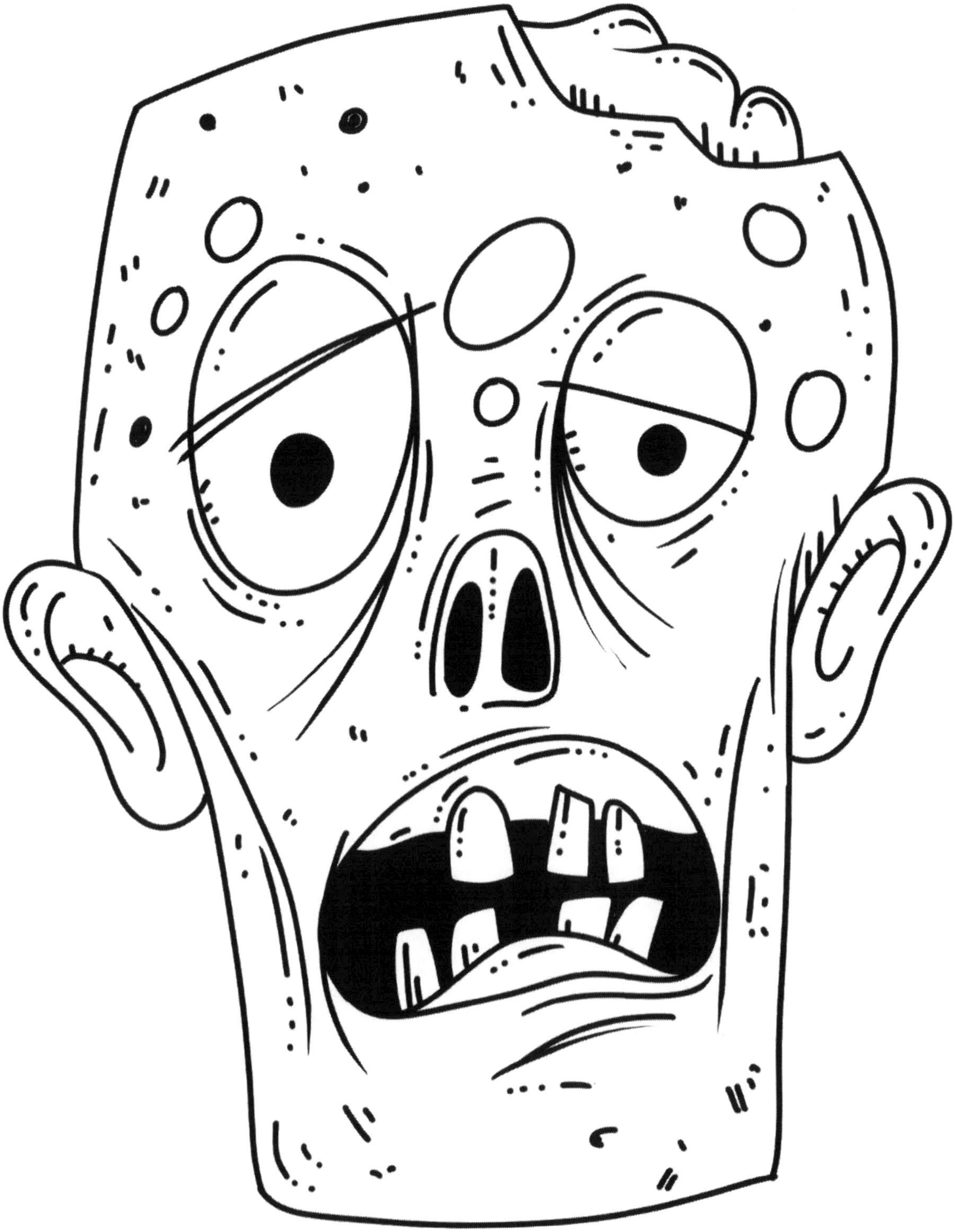

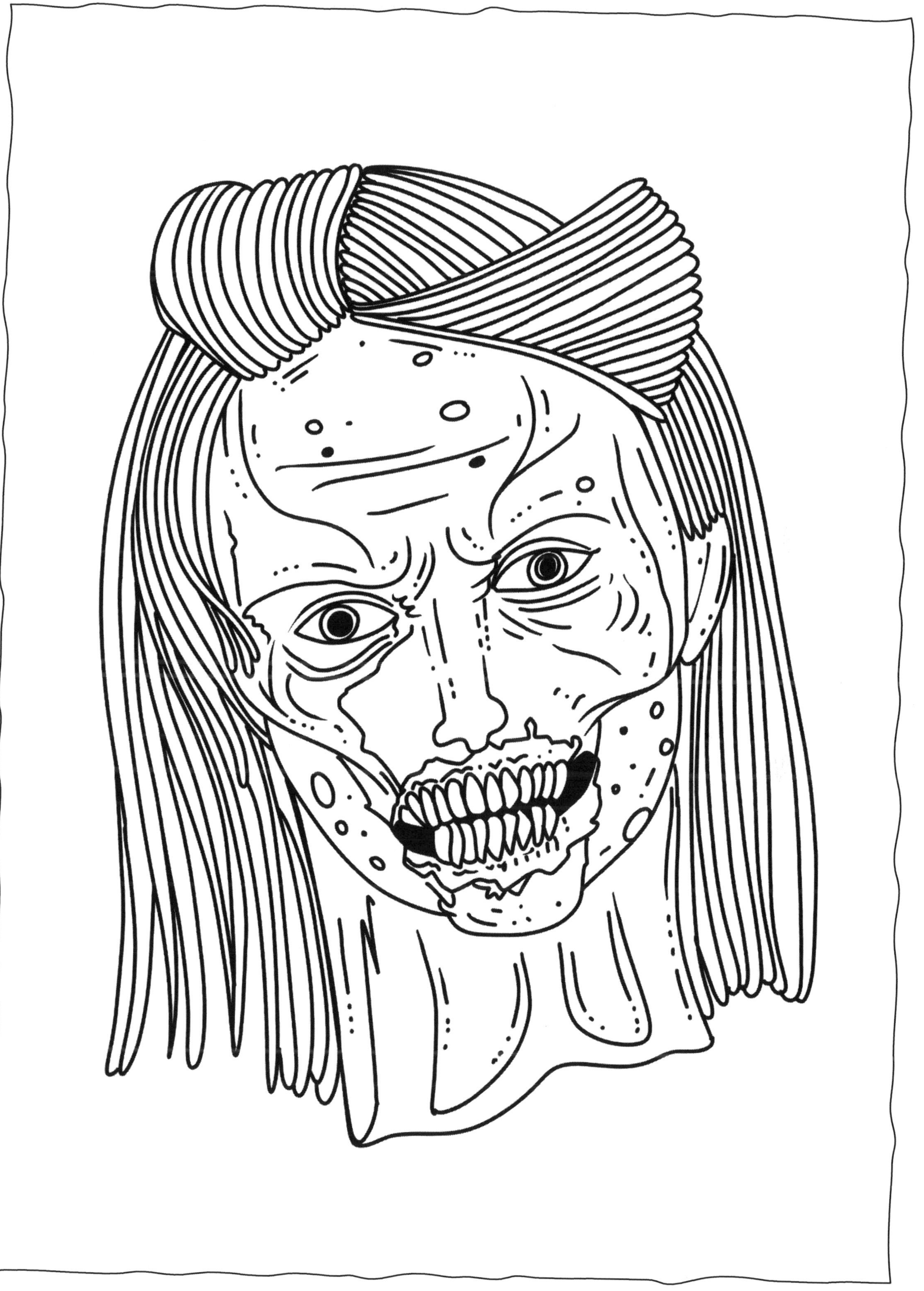

R.I.P.

Printed in Great Britain
by Amazon

48304702R00032